TROMBONE

Disney CLASSICS

T0077120

THE CD IS PLAYABLE ON ANY CD PLAYER. FOR PC AND MAC USERS, THE CD IS ENHANCED SO YOU CAN ADJUST THE RECORDING TO ANY TEMPO WITHOUT CHANGING PITCH.

The following songs are the property of:
BOURNE CO.
Music Publishers
5 West 37th Street
New York, NY 10018

Baby Mine
Give a Little Whistle
Heigh-Ho
I've Got No Strings

Some Day My Prince Will Come
When You Wish Upon a Star
Whistle While You Work
Who's Afraid of the Big Bad Wolf?

Disney characters and artwork © Disney Enterprises, Inc.

ISBN 978-1-4584-1602-5

WALT DISNEY MUSIC COMPANY
WONDERLAND MUSIC COMPANY, INC.

DISTRIBUTED BY

HAL•LEONARD® CORPORATION
7777 W. BLUEMOUND RD. P.O. BOX 13819 MILWAUKEE, WI 53213

Visit Hal Leonard Online at
www.halleonard.com

ALICE IN WONDERLAND

from Walt Disney's ALICE IN WONDERLAND

Words by BOB HILLIARD
Music by SAMMY FAIN

TROMBONE

4

BABY MINE
from Walt Disney's DUMBO

3/4

TROMBONE

Words by NED WASHINGTON
Music by FRANK CHURCHILL

Slowly, with feeling

BELLA NOTTE

(This Is the Night)

from Walt Disney's LADY AND THE TRAMP

Words and Music by PEGGY LEE
and SONNY BURKE

TROMBONE

Slowly, with feeling

GIVE A LITTLE WHISTLE

from Walt Disney's PINOCCHIO

TROMBONE

Words by NED WASHINGTON
Music by LEIGH HARLINE

HEIGH-HO

The Dwarfs' Marching Song from Walt Disney's SNOW WHITE AND THE SEVEN DWARFS

Words by LARRY MOREY
Music by FRANK CHURCHILL

9/10
TROMBONE

I'VE GOT NO STRINGS
from Walt Disney's PINOCCHIO

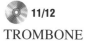
11/12

TROMBONE

Words by NED WASHINGTON
Music by LEIGH HARLINE

LITTLE APRIL SHOWER
from Walt Disney's BAMBI

TROMBONE

Words by LARRY MOREY
Music by FRANK CHURCHILL

13/14

ONCE UPON A DREAM
from Walt Disney's SLEEPING BEAUTY

15/16

TROMBONE

Words and Music by SAMMY FAIN
and JACK LAWRENCE
Adapted from a Theme by Tchaikovsky

SOME DAY MY PRINCE WILL COME

from Walt Disney's SNOW WHITE AND THE SEVEN DWARFS

17/18

TROMBONE

Words by LARRY MOREY
Music by FRANK CHURCHILL

THE UNBIRTHDAY SONG

from Walt Disney's ALICE IN WONDERLAND

19/20

TROMBONE

Words and Music by MACK DAVID,
AL HOFFMAN and JERRY LIVINGSTON

WHEN YOU WISH UPON A STAR

from Walt Disney's PINOCCHIO

21/22

TROMBONE

Words by NED WASHINGTON
Music by LEIGH HARLINE

Slowly, with feeling

WHISTLE WHILE YOU WORK

from Walt Disney's SNOW WHITE AND THE SEVEN DWARFS

Words by LARRY MOREY
Music by FRANK CHURCHILL

TROMBONE

WHO'S AFRAID OF THE BIG BAD WOLF?

from Walt Disney's THREE LITTLE PIGS

25/26

TROMBONE

Words and Music by FRANK CHURCHILL
Additional Lyric by ANN RONELL

YOU CAN FLY! YOU CAN FLY! YOU CAN FLY!

from Walt Disney's PETER PAN

Words by SAMMY CAHN
Music by SAMMY FAIN

27/28

TROMBONE